SportsZone Biographies

JOSH ALLEN

BY ANTHONY K. HEWSON

SportsZone

An Imprint of Abdo Publishing
abdobooks.com

abdobooks.com

Published by Abdo Publishing, a division of ABDO, PO Box 398166, Minneapolis, Minnesota 55439. Copyright © 2024 by Abdo Consulting Group, Inc. International copyrights reserved in all countries. No part of this book may be reproduced in any form without written permission from the publisher. SportsZone™ is a trademark and logo of Abdo Publishing.

Printed in China.
052023
092023

THIS BOOK CONTAINS
RECYCLED MATERIALS

Cover Photo: Don Juan Moore/Getty Images Sport/Getty Images
Interior Photos: Joshua Bessex/AP Images, 5; Timothy T. Ludwig/Getty Images Sport/Getty Images, 6; Ryan Kang/AP Images, 9; Tom Pennington/Getty Images Sport/Getty Images, 11; Tom Szczerbowski/Getty Images Sport/Getty Images, 13; Jerry Holt/Star Tribune/Getty Images, 14; Gregory Fisher/Icon Sportswire/Getty Images, 17; Cooper Neill/Getty Images Sport/Getty Images, 18; Adam Glanzman/Getty Images Sport/Getty Images, 21; Nic Antaya/Getty Images Sport/Getty Images, 22; Jason Hanna/Getty Images Sport/Getty Images, 25; Barry Chin/Boston Globe/Getty Images, 27; Matt Durisko/AP Images, 29

Editor: Charlie Beattie
Series Designer: Karli Kruse

LIBRARY OF CONGRESS CONTROL NUMBER: 2022949110

Publisher's Cataloging-in-Publication Data

Names: Hewson, Anthony K., author.
Title: Josh Allen / by Anthony K. Hewson
Description: Minneapolis, Minnesota: Abdo Publishing Company, 2024 | Series: SportsZone biographies | Includes online resources and index.
Identifiers: ISBN 9781098291679 (lib. bdg.) | ISBN 9781098278229 (ebook)
Subjects: LCSH: Allen, Josh, 1996--Juvenile literature. | Football players--Biography--Juvenile literature. | Quarterbacks (Football)--Biography--Juvenile literature. | Professional athletes--Biography--Juvenile literature.
Classification: DDC 796.092--dc23

TABLE OF CONTENTS

Chapter One

THE HARD ROAD

On a chilly January night, the fans at Buffalo's Highmark Stadium moved to the edges of their seats. Buffalo Bills quarterback Josh Allen was dropping back to pass. The fans had come to expect magic when the ball was in Allen's hands. And the young National Football League (NFL) star usually delivered.

It was the opening drive of a wild-card playoff game on January 15, 2022. As Allen scanned the field, he found his receivers covered. Suddenly, some New England Patriots defenders broke through the offensive line. If Allen was going to make a play, he'd have to do it with his legs.

As Bills fans knew, Allen could be a dangerous runner. The 25-year-old had made a name for himself in four seasons as a dual threat. Opponents were also aware he could make highlight-reel plays with his arm or legs. Allen swung around to the left and spotted an opening. He sprinted past two chasing Patriots before a safety eventually angled Allen

Josh Allen scrambles against the New England Patriots during the 2022 playoffs.

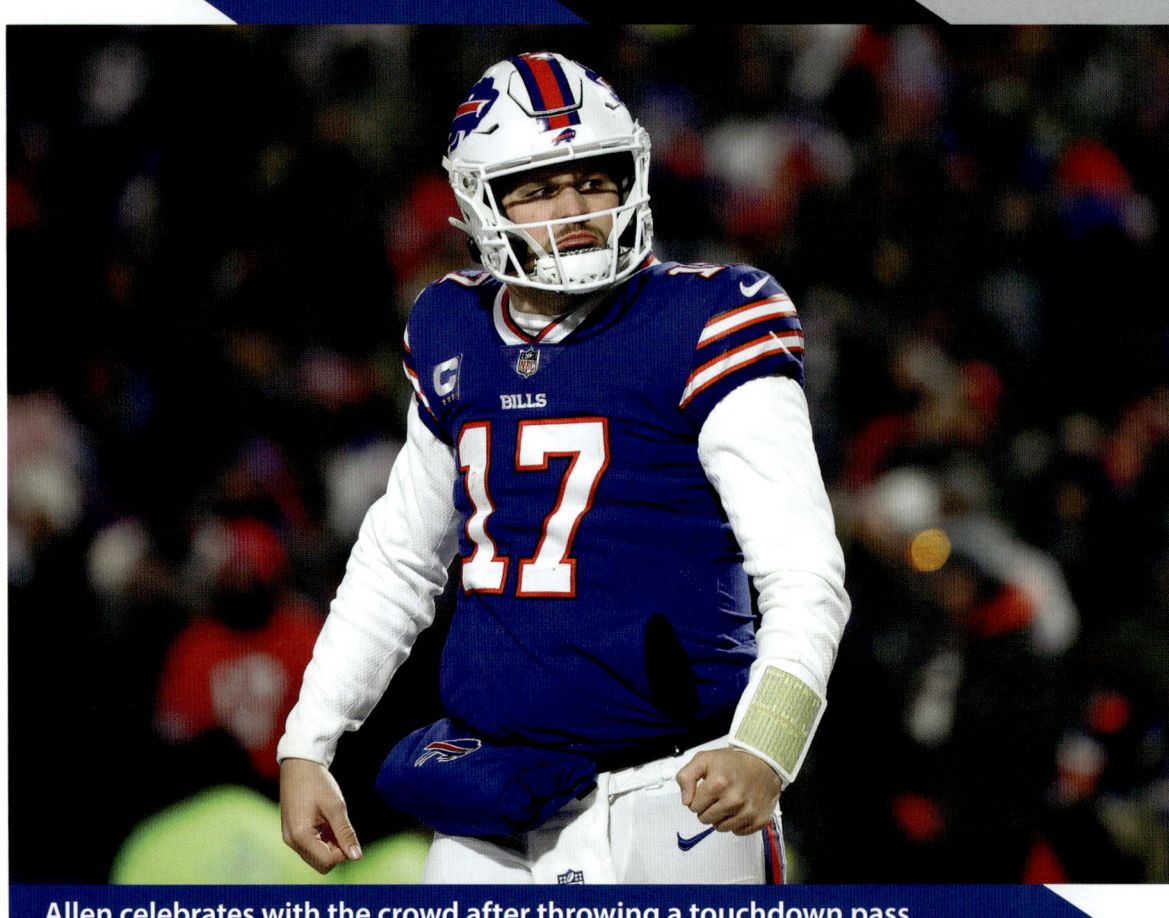

Allen celebrates with the crowd after throwing a touchdown pass against New England.

out of bounds. When the play was finally over, Allen had gained 26 yards.

A few plays later, Allen sprinted to the right for 15 more yards. That set up an 8-yard touchdown pass from Allen to tight end Dawson Knox. The Bills' touchdown drive had covered 70 yards. Their quarterback had gained 41 of them on the ground.

As the jubilant crowd watched on, Allen threw four more touchdown passes in the game. The Bills routed their division rivals 47–17. In Buffalo, fans knew their team had one of the most exciting players in the NFL. He was an icon of the city, and a household name to sports fans around the country. But just a few years earlier, hardly anyone could have predicted Allen would ever become a superstar.

FIELDS OF FIREBAUGH

Firebaugh, California, is a small farming town of just over 8,000 people. It is in a region between the Bay Area and Fresno known as the Central Valley. Allen's family had farmed the land for three generations. Josh grew up working in his family's cotton fields with his younger brother, Jason.

When he wasn't working, Josh was playing any sport he could. He played basketball, baseball, and golf as well as football. He even swam in the summertime. Allen excelled at everything, especially football. The wiry 6-foot-3-inch, 180-pound quarterback thrilled local fans with his play in high school.

The only problem for Allen was Firebaugh's size. His team played only other small schools in the area. It wasn't the kind of place college coaches came looking for future stars. As a senior, Allen didn't receive a single Division I scholarship offer. He wanted badly to play for

FAST FACT

In addition to playing multiple sports in high school, Allen also competed in Future Farmers of America (FFA). He was a national finalist in crop production.

his favorite team. Fresno State University was just down the road. But the Bulldogs weren't interested. The coaching staff told Allen they were looking for someone bigger.

Instead, Allen enrolled at Reedley College, a junior college in the area. During the 2014 season, he threw 26 touchdown passes and only five interceptions for the Tigers. He also grew into a 6-foot-5-inch, 210-pound monster of an athlete who could both throw and run.

Allen sent emails to more than 1,000 Division I college coaches that year. Only one, University of Wyoming head coach Craig Bohl, came to visit Allen's home. Bohl offered Allen a scholarship. Allen sent one last hopeful email to Fresno State. When it was rejected, he was on his way to Laramie, Wyoming.

COWBOY UP

Allen played only two games during his first year with the Cowboys. He spent most of the season out with a broken collarbone while the team went 2–10. It was only when he returned in 2016 that Allen became the starting quarterback.

The Cowboys had suffered four losing seasons in a row. Allen turned things around quickly. He threw for 3,203 yards and rushed

Allen threw for 5,066 yards and 44 touchdowns in his two years as the starting quarterback at Wyoming.

for more than 500 yards. He also tossed 28 touchdown passes. Wyoming finished 8–6 and was selected to play in a bowl game.

After initially thinking about entering the NFL Draft, Allen decided to return to Laramie. He led the Cowboys to an 8–5 record, including a bowl-game victory. Allen's personal numbers weren't that outstanding, but many NFL scouts had taken notice of his skills. Allen was no longer the small-town kid hoping for a chance. He was about to step onto the biggest football stage in the world.

Chapter Two

FROM COWBOY TO BUFFALO

During the early 1990s, the Buffalo Bills went to four straight Super Bowls. Though they lost all four, it was still an amazing feat. No other team in NFL history had gone to four straight Super Bowls. Those Bills were quarterbacked by Jim Kelly. In 11 seasons in Buffalo, Kelly rewrote the team's passing record book. He played his last game in 1996, the same year Josh Allen was born.

Fast forward to 2018, and the Bills had not won another playoff game since Kelly left. During that stretch, the team had gone through several quarterbacks. The passionate fans of Buffalo watched patiently as the Bills continued to come up short.

The Bills had the 12th pick in the 2018 NFL Draft. They needed a quarterback badly. Buffalo had reached the playoffs the year before, but its offense had been one of

Josh Allen holds up a Buffalo Bills jersey after the team drafted him in 2018.

the worst in the NFL. Only one team had passed for fewer yards than Buffalo.

Allen was one of several top quarterbacks available in the draft. The others all came from big schools. Allen had less of a track record. But when the kid from Wyoming was still available at pick number seven, the Bills pounced. They made a trade to move up and pick Allen.

While Allen had many fans, some people thought choosing him was risky. Allen hadn't played many top teams in college, and some experts wondered whether he could jump up to the best football league in the world. He had also never been a very accurate passer. Most top college quarterbacks complete over 60 percent of their passes. In three years at Wyoming, Allen had completed only 56.3 percent of his. But Allen had a rocket arm. And the Bills' coaches knew his running ability might help when the weather got cold late in the season in Buffalo. They thought it was worth taking a chance on him.

WELCOME TO THE NFL

Allen didn't become the Bills' starter right away. In his rookie training camp, he lost a competition for the job to veteran Nathan Peterman. After Peterman struggled against the Baltimore Ravens

Allen threw for 245 yards against the Los Angeles Chargers in his first NFL start.

in Week 1, Allen came on in the second half of a 47–3 defeat. The next week, Buffalo head coach Sean McDermott picked Allen as the starter against the Los Angeles Chargers. In front of a home crowd, Allen threw his first NFL touchdown pass with 38 seconds left in the game. But the Bills lost 31–20.

A week later, the Bills traveled to Minnesota to play the Vikings. Minnesota was considered a heavy favorite. Buffalo took the opening kickoff and marched 75 yards in nine plays.

Allen capped the drive with a 10-yard touchdown run, his first in the NFL.

The Bills raced out to a 17–0 lead, and they were on the move late in the first quarter. On a third-and-nine play, Allen took off running up the middle of the field. Vikings linebacker Anthony Barr positioned himself right in Allen's path. Instead of juking the linebacker, Allen hurdled Barr and picked up the first down.

Fans around the league took notice of Allen after he hurdled Minnesota Vikings linebacker Anthony Barr.

Many NFL players have the athleticism to hurdle defenders. But not many of them are quarterbacks. The play became a social media sensation after Buffalo's surprising 27–6 win. The Bills' social media team photoshopped images of Allen hopping over all kinds of objects. One had him jumping over a pair of buffalo. Another had Allen leaping over the moon. Even Kelly got in on the praise, tweeting, "I know I never would have been able to hurdle like that. Well done!"

The rest of Allen's rookie season wasn't always as smooth. He threw 20 touchdown passes but also 12 interceptions. Allen's completion percentage of 52.8 percent was the lowest in the NFL. However, he led all quarterbacks with eight rushing touchdowns, even though he missed four games due to injuries.

Though the Bills finished 6–10, Allen gave fans a glimpse into the future in the final game of the season. He threw three touchdown passes and ran for two more scores. The Bills routed the Miami Dolphins 42–17. After the season was over, Kelly called Allen "the real deal."

FAST FACT

Allen became a spokesperson for a Buffalo children's hospital in 2019. In his first year, he pledged to donate $200 for every touchdown he scored that season.

Chapter Three

WINGING IT

A llen returned to the field in 2019 with something new on his Bills uniform—a captain's C. Allen's teammates had named him one of six captains for the new season. With the team behind him, Allen set out to show his improved skills. And he needed those skills right away in the season opener.

On the road at the New York Jets, the Bills found themselves behind 16–0 in the third quarter. A field goal cut the score to 16–3. Allen and the offense got the ball back on the opening play of the fourth quarter. Allen led a drive from the Buffalo 15-yard line down to the Jets' 3-yard line in less than five minutes. He capped it off with a touchdown run.

After another defensive stop, Allen took to the air on the next drive. Starting at the Buffalo 20-yard line, Allen completed four passes to get to the Jets' 38 with 3:07 left. On third-and-four, Allen dropped back and zipped a pass down

Josh Allen reaches for the goal line on a touchdown run against the New York Jets on the opening day of the 2019 season.

Allen leaps over a Houston Texans defender during the teams' playoff matchup in January 2020.

the left sideline. Receiver John Brown hauled it in, then jogged the final few yards into the end zone. The 17–16 score held up for a comeback win.

The victory set the tone for a fun season in Buffalo. The Bills returned to the playoffs as a wild-card team by finishing 10–6. Allen was at the heart of it all. He improved his passing accuracy and threw 20 touchdowns against only nine interceptions. Allen also scored nine of the team's 13 rushing touchdowns.

Allen showed his mettle again in the playoffs. He led a 41-yard drive to set up a tying field goal late in the fourth quarter against the Houston Texans. The Bills came up short in overtime, but Bills fans knew they had a star quarterback to lean on.

BEAST OF THE EAST

No longer a question mark, Allen entered 2020 as one of the league's most exciting players. And during the season, he lived up to the hype. Allen finished fifth among all NFL quarterbacks with 4,544 passing yards and 37 touchdowns. Both marks broke Buffalo single-season records. Even better, only three quarterbacks were more accurate. In just three seasons, Allen had taken his completion rate from 52.8 percent to 69.2 percent.

With those big stats came several big wins. For two decades, the Bills had been looking up at the mighty New England Patriots. New England had won all but two American Football Conference (AFC) East division titles since 2001. The Bills hadn't won one since 1995. Behind Allen's superstar play, Buffalo finished 13–3. The Bills won the division easily.

PLAYOFF SUCCESS

The next step was ending Buffalo's 25-year drought without a playoff win. Late in the first half, the Bills trailed the Indianapolis Colts 10–7. Allen drove the Bills 96 yards in less than two minutes. He capped the drive with a five-yard touchdown run to put Buffalo ahead at halftime.

The Bills led 17–10 early in the fourth quarter when Allen had the Bills on the move again. On a first down play from the Colts' 35-yard line, Allen faked a handoff. He looked to his left, then swung his head back to the right and let loose a hard, perfect spiral. It arced just over a defender's arm and into the hands of Bills receiver Stefon Diggs in the end zone. Allen's second big play of the day helped Buffalo hold off Indianapolis for a 27–24 win.

Allen threw for 817 yards and ran for 145 more during the Bills' playoff run after the 2020 season.

A 17–3 victory over the Baltimore Ravens put the Bills in the conference championship game. It took another great quarterback to keep Allen's Bills away from the Super Bowl. Allen threw for 287 yards and rushed for a team-high 88 more against the Kansas City Chiefs. But Chiefs quarterback Patrick Mahomes was just as good. He threw for 325 yards and three touchdowns. Kansas City won 38–24.

Allen quickly built a special relationship with Buffalo fans.

HOMETOWN KID

Though Allen hadn't yet taken the Bills to the top, he had won the hearts of Buffalo fans. The cold, northern city is one of the smallest in the NFL. Outside of the Bills, Buffalo doesn't get much national attention. Not many superstars choose to play there.

Allen, on the other hand, embraced his new community from the start. He even told reporters he fell in love with the city's famous chicken wings on his first visit before he was even drafted. When others talked about the harsh winter, Allen mentioned how much he liked the spring and summer in Buffalo. The tight-knit community of Bills fans, known as the "Bills Mafia," loved Allen as much for that as for his play on the field.

Both Allen's stats and his connection to Buffalo helped him earn a huge new contract after the 2020 season. The Bills gave Allen a six-year deal that could eventually reach $258 million if he played well enough. The quarterback signed it, telling reporters that he wanted to stay in Buffalo for his entire career.

Chapter Four

CIRCLING THE WAGONS

Week 5 of the 2021 season brought a rematch for Allen and the Buffalo Bills against the Kansas City Chiefs. Early in the fourth quarter, Allen took off running to his left. One defender was in his way. Just like Anthony Barr in 2018, Kansas City cornerback L'Jarius Sneed was left grabbing nothing but air as Allen leaped right over him and kept going. The highlight play helped the Bills win 38–20.

Even as Allen improved as a passer, he still liked to take off running. Most NFL quarterbacks run only when they have to. The Bills called specific plays that allowed Allen to make something happen with his feet. And unlike some other signal callers, he didn't seem to mind getting hit. At 6 feet, 5 inches and 237 pounds, Allen often dished out as much punishment as he got.

Josh Allen attempts a pass against the Kansas City Chiefs in October 2021.

PLAYOFF PERFORMER

On the ground and in the air, Allen was again a star in 2021. He ran for a career-high 763 yards while also putting up big passing numbers. The Bills once again won their division. After the team's 47–17 pasting of the rival New England Patriots, it was time for Allen and Patrick Mahomes to duel once again.

The two young quarterbacks went back and forth all game. With just under eight minutes left, a field goal put Kansas City up 26–21. Allen went straight to work. Dodging the Chiefs' pass rush, he drove the Bills 75 yards in 17 plays. With 1:54 left, Allen hit receiver Gabe Davis on a 27-yard touchdown pass to go up 29–26.

Not to be outdone, Mahomes marched the Chiefs right back down the field. He threw a 64-yard touchdown pass with 1:02 left. The game was quickly becoming an all-time classic. Allen made sure of it by leading another 75-yard scoring drive. This time it took just six plays. The last one was a 19-yard touchdown strike to Davis with only 13 seconds remaining.

FAST FACT

On November 7, 2021, Josh Allen was sacked by Josh Allen. The Jacksonville Jaguars defensive end sharing Allen's name also intercepted a pass. It was the first time an NFL player had been sacked by or intercepted by a player with the same name.

Allen (17) celebrates with his offensive line after throwing one of his five touchdown passes against the New England Patriots on January 15, 2022.

The dramatic touchdown seemed certain to have won the game. But Kansas City gained 44 yards on just two plays. A field goal tied the game on the final snap of regulation. The teams were headed to overtime tied 36–36.

Allen had played nearly perfect football all night. He had thrown for 329 yards and four touchdowns. He led the Bills with 68 rushing yards. As the road captain, it was Allen's job to call the overtime coin toss. He guessed wrong, and the Chiefs got the ball.

Allen never got off the sideline. Mahomes took Kansas City down the field for the winning score. Since Kansas City scored a touchdown, NFL rules stated the game was over. Afterward, the two young superstars shook hands on the field. Both knew it was a special game they had just played in.

The ending angered many NFL observers. For days fans and media members vented their frustration that the Bills didn't get a chance to play offense in overtime. Many wanted the NFL to alter its rules so that such a situation never happened again. The league listened. Starting the next year, any overtime playoff game would see both teams getting a shot on offense.

The Bills had once again come up short of the Super Bowl. But it was hard to fault Buffalo's quarterback. In two playoff games, he had thrown for 637 yards and nine touchdowns without an interception.

Allen and the Bills were great once again in 2022, finishing 13–3. However, they bowed out in the divisional round again. This time Buffalo lost 27–10 to the Cincinnati Bengals. It was another disappointing end for a fan base that wanted nothing more than a Super Bowl title.

Allen attempts a pass in a heavy snowstorm during the Bills' playoff game against the Cincinnati Bengals in January 2023.

However, those same fans knew they could show up every Sunday and watch one of the best quarterbacks in the league. Allen was capable of making something special happen anytime he touched the ball. He was 26 years old and wanted to play in Buffalo for life. There was plenty of time left to bring the city the ultimate NFL prize.

GLOSSARY

comeback
When one team that was losing rallies to tie or win.

contract
An agreement to play for a certain team.

division
A smaller group of teams within a league.

draft
A system that allows teams to acquire new players coming into a league.

drought
A long period without success.

favorite
The person or team that is expected to win.

junior college
A two-year college that often includes athletic programs.

overtime
An extra period of play when the score is tied after regulation.

pasting
A severe defeat.

rookie
A professional athlete in his or her first year of competition.

scholarship
Money awarded to a student to pay for educational expenses.

scout
A person whose job is to look for talented young players.

walk-on
A college athlete who does not receive a scholarship for participating.

MORE INFORMATION

BOOKS

Flynn, Brendan. *The NFL Encyclopedia*. Minneapolis, MN: Abdo Reference, 2022.

Graves, Will. *GOATs of Football*. Minneapolis, MN: Abdo Publishing, 2022.

Hewson, Anthony K. *Patrick Mahomes*. Minneapolis, MN: Abdo Publishing, 2024.

ONLINE RESOURCES

To learn more about Josh Allen, please visit **abdobooklinks.com** or scan this QR code. These links are routinely monitored and updated to provide the most current information available.

INDEX

ABOUT THE AUTHOR

Anthony K. Hewson is a freelance writer originally from San Diego. He and his wife now live in the San Francisco Bay Area with their two dogs.